Rochester

in old picture postcards

by
Alan Moss
and
Kevin Russell

European Library – Zaltbommel/Netherlands

Acknowledgements:

The authors gratefully acknowledge the assistance given in the preparation of this book by: Mr. M. Moad, curator, and the staff of the Guildhall Museum, Rochester; Graham and Linda West, Medway Stamp Centre, High Street, Rochester; Mrs. L. Chambers, Mr. R.E. Head, Mr. R. Lambert, Mr. E.C. Moss, Mrs. P.J. Moss, Miss F. Nixey, Mr. and Mrs. R.F. Russell and Mrs. S. Smith.

GB ISBN 90 288 4700 6 / CIP

INTRODUCTION

Rochester has the unusual distinction of being a city within a city. When local government was being re-organised in the early 1970s it presented officialdom with a problem: it was too large to be relegated to the status of a civil parish, but not quite large enough to become a district in its own right. It was therefore amalgamated with the adjoining borough of Chatham and with the rural parishes of the Hoo Peninsular to form the new borough of Medway. But 2,000 years of history could not be cast aside to satisfy the transient needs of the administrators and, by Special Letters Patent, Her Majesty The Queen granted to Rochester the right to go on calling itself a city. After further deliberation by local councillors it was decided to change the name of the borough from Medway to Rochester upon Medway, and in due course Her Majesty consented to the grant of another charter which gave city status to the whole area.

Although, therefore, the name Rochester upon Medway is a very recent creation, and applies to an administrative area of some 62 square miles stretching from the North Downs to the Thames Estuary, it also aptly describes the ancient city itself which grew out of a settlement whose origins are lost in the mists of time but which owed its very existence to the river. In earlier times the Medway was a broader and shallower stream than it is today and it was possible to cross the bed of the river at the point where today bridges carry unending streams of motor traffic. The highway which crosses the Medway at Rochester was an ancient track even before the Romans arrived. A convenient route for travellers heading west from the coast, it avoided the densely forested area to the south which we know as the Weald of Kent. Watling Street, as the road became known, was an important artery in the network of highways which covered Roman Britain and the crossing of the Medway was an important point on that highway; too important to be subject to the vagaries of wind and tide. Hence the first bridge was built here during the Roman occupation and the primitive riverside settlement developed into Durobrivae, a fortified town of no small significance.

The city's first recorded Christian church was established early in the seventh century by Bishop Justus only a few years after St. Augustine had arrived at Canterbury. However, the so-called dark ages which followed the departure of the Romans from our shores were dark indeed for Rochester and its Christian community. Sited on the banks of a river which flows directly into the North Sea, the city was easy prey for raiding parties from the low countries and Scandinavia, and it is believed that the little cathedral church was destroyed and rebuilt, along with the city it served, on more than one occasion.

The strategic value of Rochester's position was obvious to the Normans and work was under way soon after the Conquest of 1066 to re-vitalise the city's defences. The first castle, a wooden structure, appears to have had a fairly short life and in about 1087 the first Norman bishop, Gundulph, was charged with the task of building a new castle. At much the same time this energetic man, the 'builder-bishop' as he is sometimes known, was also creating a new cathedral and priory, dedicated to St. Andrew, to replace the run down Anglo-Saxon establishment. Both castle and cathedral were completed after his death, and have been extensively altered since then, but it is to Bishop Gundulph that we owe the two features which still dominate the skyline and which are the very heart of the city.

For centuries Rochester's growth was slow, its population being very largely contained within its medieval bounds, with ribbons of development extending eastwards towards St. Bartholomew's Hospital (another of Bishop Gundulph's foundations), westwards across the river in Strood, and southwards along St.Margaret's Street. However, the late eighteenth and nineteenth centuries saw rapid growth and with it the gradual extension of the city's boundaries into the surrounding parishes. Part of Strood near the bridge had lain within the city's jurisdiction since 1460, but after 1835 that jurisdiction was extended so that eventually it was to embrace the whole of the urban area west of the Medway.

The influx of new people was brought about to a large extent by the expansion of the naval and military establishments in the area, particularly the extension of nearby Chatham Dockyard, and by industrial growth. Cement was in great demand and new works sprang up along the banks of the Medway taking advantage of the abundant chalk deposits in the area. Industrial development was of course greatly facilitated by the arrival of the railways, the first line reaching the city at Strood in 1846.

Charles Dickens observed, and regretted, many of these changes. His family had come to live at Chatham in 1817 and his abiding affection for the area, and for Rochester in particular, is reflected in many of his writings. The unfinished story of Edwin Drood, for example, contains a wonderfully evocative description of the old city (which Dickens calls 'Cloisterham') written very shortly before he died at his home at Gads Hill.

The changes which were already taking place during Charles Dickens' lifetime have gone on apace ever since. Two world wars, industrial growth, and sudden decline, a vastly increased population and above all the insatiable demands of the motor car, have all left their physical marks, while changes in the economic and social order have left marks of another and perhaps more far reaching kind. Yet despite everything, the old city has come through to the last quarter of the twentieth century remarkably unscathed.

In this small collection of pictures, covering the late nineteenth and early twentieth centuries, there is much that will be familiar to the newcomer but also much that will stir memories among older residents of the way things were the day before yesterday.

Alan Moss
Kevin Russell

1. The coat of arms of the City of Rochester. Comprising a simple shield in red and gold and displaying the Lion of England and the letter 'r', its existence as a seal device was first recorded in 1574. Four hundred years later new armorial bearings were created for the new administrative area incorporating elements of the arms of the City of Rochester, the Borough of Chatham and the Rural District of Strood. This representation of Rochester's arms is reproduced from an early twentieth century postcard – one of a series on heraldic devices.

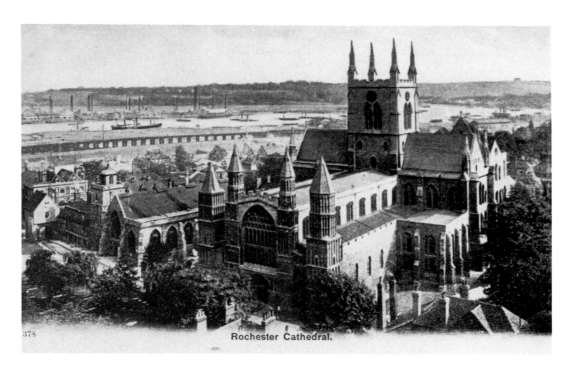

378

Rochester Cathedral.

2. Emerging from the stone staircase that winds its way to the top of the keep of Rochester Castle, one is rewarded with a breathtaking panorama of town, river and countryside which, over the years, has attracted countless artists, photographers and casual sight-seers. In this classic view, taken just after the turn of the century, the photographer has captured a scene which is both instantly recogniseable and yet so very different today. In any comparison with a modern photograph the most obvious difference is the altered appearance of the cathedral, but looking more closely one can see where other changes have taken place. The cement factories have long gone, as has the curious little branch railway line which ran, parallel to the main Dover line, for a mere 1 1/2 miles from Strood junction to a station called Chatham Central but which was in fact in Rochester.

3. Moving one's position slightly from that in the previous picture reveals another aspect of the view from the castle. In this shot, taken a few years after the preceding one, the reason for the castle's existence, to defend the crossing of the River Medway, can clearly be seen. The view is full of the stark contrasts of Victorian and Edwardian England. The opulent houses, then only just completed, on Castle Hill, and the fragile bandstand (the latter now demolished) represent one aspect, while the terraces of more humble dwellings, the factories and the sailing barges on the Strood side of the river, represent another. On the distant hilltop are three of the windmills which were once such a common site around the town. The civic centre, headquarters of Rochester upon Medway City Council, now occupies the site of Aveling and Porter's road locomotive works to the left of the bridge.

4. Rochester's first cathedral was built in 604 by St. Justus, a missionary sent from Canterbury by St. Augustine. It was a tiny building and stood near the west end of the present cathedral. The Normans found the church in Rochester at the time of the conquest to be very run down and, under the direction of a new bishop, Gundulph, set about building the new cathedral and priory of St. Andrew. Work started in about 1080 and the building was consecrated on Ascension Day 1130. The choir was added in the 13th century and a tower with spire was raised in 1343. By the 19th century the years of post-Reformation neglect had taken their toll and extensive repairs and restoration work had to be carried out. In 1823 the spire was removed to take the weight off the tower, which was later remodelled and surmounted by the four pinnacles as seen in this late-Victorian view.

Rochester Cathedral

5. This photograph, taken only a few short years after the last one, shows clearly the striking difference in the appearance of the cathedral brought about by the re-building of the tower and the restoration of the spire in 1904. The work was carried out at the expense of Mr. Thomas Hellyar Foord, and was the culmination of almost a century of work which had rescued the cathedral from near ruin. Nestling under the north wall of the nave is a little cemetery which provided a source of inspiration to Charles Dickens. The author, who was a frequent visitor to the city, took note of some of the names on the gravestones and wove characters around them which later appeared in his famous novels.

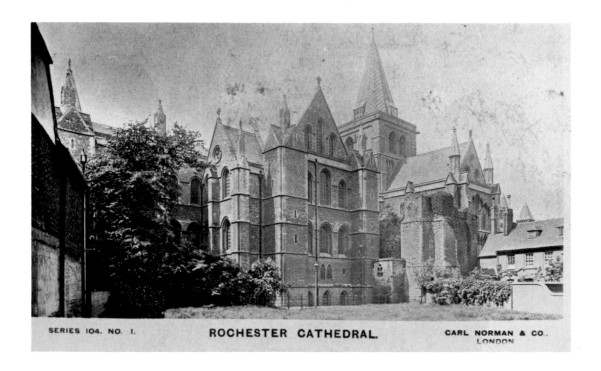

ROCHESTER CATHEDRAL.

6. When Bishop Gundulph began building the present cathedral, one of his first tasks was to build a stronghold from the protection of which the work could proceed. The remains of Gundulph's Tower still stand as a witness to those turbulent years following the Norman Conquest, when the Conqueror's men were still securing their hold over the English people. In this Edwardian view the tower can be seen right of centre partly covered with creeper. By this time it had been cut down by about one third of its original height. The open space in the foreground, known as St. Mary's Meadow and once occupied by part of the old priory of St. Andrew, has since been landscaped and now contains the city's war memorial.

7. Although altered and restored in succeeding centuries the late Norman west front is one of the glories of Rochester Cathedral and one of the best of its type in England. The main doorway contains some fine sculptures of that period, while the window above, inserted in 1470, was restored by the Victorians as a memorial to the Royal Engineers who fought and died in the Afghan and South African wars. The regiment is garrisoned in the Medway Towns and claims a direct line of descent from Gundulph, the great Norman 'builder bishop' of Rochester. The iron railings, of which our Victorian forebears seem to have been so fond, added a sombre and somewhat unwelcoming touch to the approach to the cathedral. Most of the railings have now disappeared and one cannot mourn their passing.

8. The west door of Rochester Cathedral provides a splendid background against which to show off the new family car. The proud owner, Mr. John Benjamin Frith and family, pose for the cameraman in their 1912 G.W.K. type, 8 h.p. grey two seater motor car. Mr. Frith kept a well-known pharmacy in the High Street for many years. However, the car had a brief life ending its days in 1916, after passing through the hands of three more owners, all incidentally military gentlemen within the locality. The somewhat plain car body is enhanced by the large brass single headlight mounted in the centre of the radiator, the two smaller side lamps and the horn!

9. The pilgrims' steps in the cathedral lead up to the north choir transept where, until the Reformation, stood the shrine of St. William of Perth. William, a baker by trade, was murdered near the city in the year 1201 while en route from his native Scotland to the Holy Land. His body was buried by the monks in the cathedral where it became the object of veneration. All such shrines and relics were ruthlessly destroyed in the years following the break with Rome, and today virtually nothing remains of William's tomb. Nothing, that is, except these steps, the treads of which are so worn by the feet (or knees) of those pilgrims of long ago that boards have been placed across them to make them safe to walk on.

PILGRIMS STEPS, ROCHESTER CATHEDRAL. K.3040.

Rochester Cathedral   The Nave

10. Standing inside the west door of the cathedral one's eye is drawn first to the massive pillars of Gundulph's nave and then to the organ screen, the design of which is relatively modern. The organ case was re-built by Sir George Gilbert Scott in 1878 and the grouping of the pipes in two turrets enables one's eye to travel the length of the quire to the very end of the building. Below the organ is a group of eight statues representing St. Andrew, St. Justus, Bishop Gundulph, and others with a special place in the cathedral's history. They were placed there in 1890 in memory of Dean Scott. The heavily ornamented font in the foreground was given in memory of Canon Burrows, who died in 1892. It has since been removed to a position between the first and second pillars on the right of the nave.

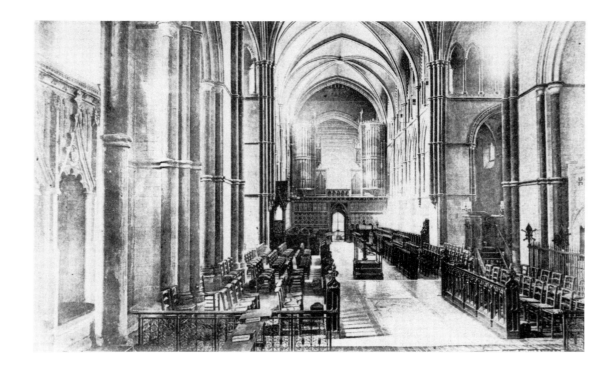

11. The shrine of St. William proved to be a new and valuable source of income to the monks who used the money brought by the pilgrims to extend the cathedral. A new quire was opened in 1227, followed later in the century by the north and south transepts. In their enthusiasm for renewal, the monks planned, and had commenced, the re-building of the rest of the cathedral. However, the money ran out and much of Gundulph's original nave survives to this day. As seen in this late Victorian picture the choir shows the results of the extensive work of restoration carried out by Gilbert Scott and others in the nineteenth century. The lectern in the centre of the aisle has since been removed to a position in the left foreground.

12. The Chapter House doorway, leading off the south choir transept, is one of the architectural treasures of Rochester Cathedral. Dating from the mid-fourteenth century it is elaborately decorated with figures representing the triumph of the Christian church over Judaism. During the Cromwellian era the carvings were damaged, the largest figures to left and right of the door losing their heads. During restoration in the early nineteenth century the left hand figure received the male head seen in this picture. Historical research, however, proved this to be incorrect and a new, female, head has adorned her shoulders since 1897.

Crypt, Rochester Cathedral

13. Rochester Cathedral has one of the finest Norman crypts, or under-crofts, in England, parts of which date back to the eleventh century. During the nineteenth century, when much repair and restoration work was going on, the workmen frequently used the crypt for the storage of building materials and to dump rubbish. This was probably the source of the earthy odour which pervaded the building in those days and which is mentioned more than once in the writings of Charles Dickens. The crypt was restored and re-paved in about 1897 and it would seem that the work was still in progress when this photograph was taken.

DEANERY   ROCHESTER

14. Tucked in close behind the east end of the cathedral is this elegant eighteenth century house. For many years it was the residence of the Deans of Rochester and, in this turn-of-the-century view, the Dean and his lady enjoy the peace and tranquility of its extensive garden. In more recent times the house has served as a theological college for the training of new priests. It now serves in two roles: on the upper floors are apartments for cathedral staff, while on the ground floor the St. Andrew's Visitors' Centre dispenses rest and refreshment for tourists and other visitors to the city and the cathedral. The Dean of Rochester between 1887 and 1904 was Samuel Reynolds Hole who, besides being responsible for the later stages of the cathedral's restoration, found fame as the founder of the National Rose Society.

ROCHESTER CASTLE AND GARDENS.

15. Rochester was a fortified town in Roman times, but it was William the Conqueror's men in the eleventh century who set about building the castle as we know it today. The keep was completed by William de Corbeil, Archbishop of Canterbury, in 1127. Repairs were carried out after it came under seige in 1215 and again in 1264, but very little was done to it after the mid-fourteenth century and it gradually fell into decay. Attempts were made to demolish it, but mercifully it survived, and its future was secured when in the 1870s it was leased, and later purchased by Rochester Corporation. More recent conflicts are also represented by the armaments on display in this 1920s view. The cannon in the centre background, a relic of the Crimean war, is still to be seen in the castle gardens.

Rochester Castle and Grounds

16. The grounds of Rochester Castle were laid out as a public park in the 1870s and ever since have proved to be an immensely popular asset to the city. It is a safe place for children to play while their elders stroll the wide paths or simply sit and chat. For the youngsters in the foreground of this tranquil Edwardian scene, play has temporarily ceased while they gaze at the man with the camera. The gardens themselves display the profusion of trees and shrubs many of which were later uprooted to make room for the great historical pageant which was staged here in 1931. The stone column to the left of the picture was erected as a tribute to Queen Victoria, but that too has long since vanished.

17. For these little girls, as for generations of other young visitors to the castle gardens, a popular pastime was feeding the birds. A few pence would buy a bag of corn from the caretaker's house in one of the old stone towers, and immediately one became the centre of attention for the flocks of pigeons and other wild birds which nested in the trees and in the nooks and crannies of the old castle keep. Even the peacocks which strutted proudly round the immaculate lawns and flower beds demanded their share. Times change: the flower beds and the peacocks are gone, and the pigeons are discouraged from nesting in the castle, but at least today's youngsters have the freedom to run and play on the grass, which was firmly denied to these children.

TANK PRESENTATION   ROCHESTER   2-8-19.   3

18. In 1919 the Army Council presented the city with a tank in recognition of Rochester's contribution to the war effort. The tank (No 58) which had seen service at the battle of the Somme arrived by rail and was driven through the High Street to the castle gardens in a procession which included detachments from the Royal Navy, Royal Marines, Royal West Kent and Royal Berkshire regiments. The formal presentation was made by General Sir Herbert Mullaly to the Mayor, Colonel Breton. The tank is seen here in the castle gardens with some members of the band of the Royal Berkshire Regiment. The building on the right, now demolished, served variously as the Liberal Club (for which purpose it had been built), the Castle Repertory Theatre, and finally as a police station.

19. Ten years on, and the castle gardens were the scene of a totally different sort of gathering. In June 1929 a fete was organised by the local branch of the Association for Befriending Women and Girls, and Miss (later Dame) Sybil Thorndike was invited to declare it open. The famous actress had spent much of her childhood in Rochester and was soon to become the first woman to receive the freedom of the city. She is pictured arriving for the opening ceremony with, on the left, the Mayor of Chatham. They are being welcomed on the dais by the Mayor of Rochester, Councillor 'Freddie' Matthews. Two years later Sybil Thorndike was to return to the castle gardens to take part, as 'the Spirit of Rochester', in the city's historical pageant.

20. Having watched the city's history unfold for more than 900 years, the castle was the setting for a great pageant held in June 1931 in celebration of that history. The whole city was en fête for a week, with townsfolk from all walks of life taking part. The performances, which were watched by huge crowds from stands specially erected for the occasion, were attended by celebrities such as H.R.H. Prince George, later Duke of Kent, and the Lord Mayor of London. The scene being enacted in this picture commemorated the visit of Queen Elizabeth I to the city in 1573. The part of the Queen was played by Mrs. H. Edmeades, while that of the Earl of Leicester was played by Lord Darnley, of Cobham Hall, one of the promoters of this unprecedented and highly successful event.

REBUILDING ROCHESTER BRIDGE

21. By the end of the nineteenth century it was becoming apparent that Sir William Cubitt's bridge of 1856, designed to ease the passage of both road and river traffic, was itself becoming a hazard to navigation: its elegant arches simply did not leave enough headroom for modern vessels. An ingeneous solution to the problem was devised whereby the weight of the bridge was transferred to new steel supports placed above the deck, thus allowing Cubitt's original cast iron arches to be removed. Traffic continued to use the bridge throughout its re-construction, but at a speed of no more than two miles per hour, and the passengers on the top deck of a tram crossing from Strood to Rochester were able to get a good view of the work then in progress when this photograph was taken in February 1913.

Rochester Bridge opened by Lady Darnley 14.5.14
(886)

22. The ceremonies were over, the Countess of Darnley and the other dignitaries had retired and the bunting was being removed when the photographer captured this scene on 14th May 1914. The re-modelled bridge was, however, obviously still an object of considerable interest to the local populace, many of whom had stayed behind to admire and discuss this masterpiece of modern engineering. Apart from the removal of the tram lines and the replacement of gas with electric lighting the bridge itself looks much the same today. However, in the late 1960s a second bridge was built on the piers of the old London, Chatham and Dover Railway bridge which can be seen through the arch on the right of this picture. Only Strood – bound traffic now uses the old bridge. The building on the extreme right was a victim of the road improvements of the 1960s.

Rochester Castle and River Medway

23. On a rising tide a heavily laden Thames sailing barge drifts gently clear of Rochester Bridge on a sunny day just before the First World War. The man known as the 'Huffler' has rowed out from the pier and is helping the regular crew of two to re-set the mast and sails. Hundreds of these famous vessels plied the rivers and coastal waters of eastern England, carrying goods of every description, until they were displaced by more modern modes of transport in the middle years of this century. Many have since found new uses, however: some are permanently moored as riverside homes while others have been meticulously restored and can still be seen from time to time gracing the waters of the Kent and Essex coasts.

New Bridge and Pier Rochester. (874)

24. Several years later another barge, this one belonging to Associated Portland Cement Manufacturers, brings its cargo down from one of the many cement works further up-stream. Taking advantage of the falling tide it glides slowly past Spinks's boat yard and the Esplanade Pier one day in the early 1920s. The little iron pier, which at the time of writing serves as the approach to a permanently moored restaurant ship, was in those days a useful landing stage for local boat owners, and was the place where, for a few pence, one could hire a skiff or a rowing boat for an afternoon. The raft with its hut and diving stages belonged to the Medway Swimming Club and had, somewhat surprisingly, been built at Short Brothers' aircraft works half a mile or so further up the river.

25. Swimming in the River Medway was popular in days gone by, and between the wars several clubs existed to cater for the hardy souls who wished to indulge in that somewhat hazardous pastime. One such was the Medway Swimming Club, some of whose members are seen here posing for the camera on Rochester Pier one summer day in 1919. Although ladies were catered for in the M.S.C., segregation was still the order of the day, and while the men occupied the main raft (seen in the preceding picture) the ladies had to make do with a boat moored nearby. A new municipal swimming bath opened just before the outbreak of the Second World War; this, and changing social conditions, seems more than anything else to have brought about the end of organised river swimming.

Waterplane Works, Rochester. (877)

26. This 1914 view shows the original Esplanade works of Messrs. Short Brothers, built on Tower Fields adjoining the River Medway. These world famous manufacturers of aeroplanes had acquired the site the previous year, their works at Eastchurch on the Isle of Sheppey having proved unsuitable for the construction of flying boats. The works were greatly expanded between the wars, although during the 'Depression' the company was forced to diversify, and produced light-weight bus bodies, a few tramcar bodies, entire trolley buses and even some metal sailing barges, in an effort to keep going. The late 1930s saw production of the famous 'Empire' flying boats for Imperial Airways and during the last war Stirling bombers and Sunderland and Shetland flying boats were built here. The Esplanade site, however, proved too cramped for modern aircraft production and the factory closed in July 1948, production having been transferred to Belfast.

27. Standing on the slip-way outside Short Bros. aircraft works is the 'Singapore' flying boat in which Sir Alan and Lady Cobham were to fly the 20,000 miles to Capetown in November 1927. The craft was the first all-metal flying boat to be built in Great Britain and was powered by two Rolls Royce Condor engines, each developing 700 horsepower. Accompanied by Captain H.V. Worrall as second pilot, two Rolls Royce engineers and a film cameraman, they set off from Rochester, flying first to Southampton, then across Europe to Cairo and down the length of Africa following the course of the Nile. The main purpose of the journey was to explore the possibility of establishing a regular air service from Cairo to the Cape.

Rochester   *St. Nicholas Church*

28. During the middle ages the citizens of Rochester worshipped at the altar of St. Nicholas in the cathedral. Relations between the city and the priory are said to have been uneasy however, and on 18th December 1423 a new church, also dedicated to St. Nicholas, was consecrated. Extensively renovated in the seventeenth century, it served as the parish church for the townsfolk of Rochester until the 1960s, by which time there had been a substantial shift of population away from the city centre to the outer parishes. It then assumed two roles, that of diocesan office and a bookshop, the latter use having recently ceased. Conversion to these new uses included the removal of the door at the foot of the tower, seen in this 1920s view, and the insertion of display windows.

29. Rochester's guildhall dates from 1687 and is the place where, in Charles Dickens' book 'Great Expectations', Pip was bound apprentice to Joe Gargery, the blacksmith. In its early days a produce market was held in the arcade, and this late Victorian view shows the former market place still enclosed by the iron railings which were later removed to Eastgate House. The building on the left is the former Duke's Head inn which had been acquired by the council in 1864. It was demolished in 1893 and a new wing built, at the cost of £3.000, to provide additional council offices and also to accommodate the city's new technical institute. The institute's stay there was brief, however, for in 1897 it was removed to new premises in Eastgate. Today the guildhall houses the city's museum, although the council still meets in full session in its elegant courtroom.

THE GUILDHALL, ROCHESTER.

30. 'Good House, nice beds' was how Mr. Jingle summed up the Bull Hotel in Charles Dickens' 'Pickwick Papers'. Rochester's famous coaching inn also found favour with Royalty when, in 1835, the young Princess Victoria and her mother, the Duchess of Kent, sought overnight shelter here from a storm, the ferocity of which made it unwise for the heiress to the throne to continue her journey. Today the hotel proudly bears the name Royal Victoria and Bull Hotel in honour of that visit, but in this turn-of-the-century view it was still proclaiming itself simply as the Bull. Beneath the name can be seen the letters ER which formed part of the decorations for King Edward's coronation. If the Bull represents the era of the horse-drawn coach, the little sign on the right of the picture represents that other mode of travel which has vanished just as surely from the city's streets: the electric tramcar.

31. Likened by Charles Dickens to a place where time carries on his business and hangs out his sign, Rochester's old Corn Exchange has watched over the comings and goings along the High Street since the early eighteenth century. It was erected on the site of an earlier town hall, at the expense of Sir Cloudesley Shovel, MP. Built as the entrance to a butchers' market, it takes its name from the dealings of the corn merchants who in due course displaced the butchers. For a time during the early years of this century the building served as Rochester's first cinema. Somewhat dowdy in appearance in this between-the-wars view, it has since been extensively restored and now presents a much brighter face to the world.

32. Unusually described as 'Westgate' in this early twentieth century view, 'Chertsey's Gate', as it is more commonly known, is one of the three remaining gateways to the old Priory of St. Andrew, established by Bishop Gundulph in the eleventh century. The gateway itself dates from the fifteenth century, the little wooden house above having been added in the eighteenth. This was the home of John Jasper, the cathedral choirmaster in Dickens' book 'The mystery of Edwin Drood'. The shop adjoining the gateway also featured in the story as the home of Mr. Tope, the chief verger of the cathedral.

33. This photograph shows the interior of the house wherein dwelt the fictional Tope and his wife. They occupied the upper rooms while the ground floor was rented out as lodgings. The house has, for many years, served as a restaurant. Once, as in this view taken early this century, it was known as 'Ye Old Gate House Tea Shoppe'. More recently it has come to be known simply as 'Mr. Tope's'. Dickens is said to have based the character of Mr. Tope on William Miles, who served as head verger of the cathedral from 1847 until he retired in 1892 at the age of 84.

34. The postcard reproduced here was sent by a visitor to the city in 1908. The scene depicted, however, is one which would be instantly recogniseable to today's tourist. In the intervening period the High Street, which forms part of the Roman 'Watling Street', has seen its traffic increase to intolerable levels and then, with the opening of new roads, die away again to little more than that shown here. Unfortunately the 'Royal Lifeboat' inn, on the left, was demolished shortly after this picture was taken, and with it two of the three gables in that delightful little row. 'The King's Head' still survives, however, as does the 'Northgate Inn' opposite, the latter as a restaurant rather than a public house, and Mr. Jenkins the fishmonger (extreme left) has made way for a florist.

35. The shop-keepers and owners of property in Rochester High Street made sure that this part of the city at least was well dressed for King George V's coronation and the presence of several military personnel, most of whom seem to be making their way back towards the barracks at Chatham, suggests that the photograph was taken shortly after the official celebrations in Rochester Cathedral. Among the changes which have since taken place, the tea shop on the left has been demolished and re-built, happily in similar style, although without its distinctive wrought iron balcony.

Seven Poor Travellers' Rest,
Rochester

36. Rochester High Street on an Edwardian summer's day. The open top tram is coming from Strood towards Chatham and is outside the Gordon Hotel. The white stone-faced building on the right with the large lamp over the door is the Six Poor Travellers' House, home of a charity set up by Richard Watts, Member of Parliament for Rochester in Elizabeth I's reign. By his will of 1579, this house, then an almshouse for the accommodation of elderly ladies, was enlarged and equipped to give overnight lodging to six poor travellers who could not afford to stay at the many inns along this road. The house was immortalised by Charles Dickens in his tale 'The Seven Poor Travellers', Dickens portraying himself as the seventh.

DORMITORY GALLERY, WATT'S CHARITY, ROCHESTER.

37. This delightful little courtyard is at the back of the Poor Travellers' House with, on the right, the galleried dormitory added to the main building under the will of Richard Watts. Each of the rooms has a fireplace and contained a bed with flock mattress, a chair and a Bible; luxury indeed for poor wayfarers in the sixteenth century. On the extreme left can be seen part of the weatherboarded extension, built in the nineteenth century as a dining room. Poor travellers continued to be welcomed here, in accordance with the founder's will, right up to the Second World War. In recent years the building has been beautifully restored and opened to public view as a tribute to the vision and compassion of Mr. Richard Watts.

38. The late nineteenth century buildings of Sir Joseph Williamson's Mathematical School dominated the Eastgate area of the High Street until their demolition in 1969. Enclosed within the buildings was a long section of the medieval city wall, which has since been restored and incorporated into a landscaped area fronting on to a car park built on the former school site. The Mathematical School was opened in 1709 to educate sons of freemen of the city in ways which would fit them for a nautical career. After the school had been enlarged several times it was moved in 1969 to its present site in Maidstone Road.

Rochester. Eastgate House.

39. Standing near the site of the east gate of the old walled city, Eastgate House has imposed its dignified presence on the narrow High Street since it was built by Sir Peter Buck, an important official at the nearby Chatham Naval Dockyard, in 1591. To this day it carries the sign of the buck in the square panel beneath the left-hand chimney stack. Among its various roles has been that of a school for young ladies and as such is mentioned in the writings of Charles Dickens. It was the city's museum from 1897 until 1979 and now serves as part of the Charles Dickens Centre. In this view, in which the cameraman has aroused the curiosity of a number of passers-by, the Foord Annexe, built in 1923 at the expense of Mr. Thomas Hellyer Foord as an extension to the museum, has yet to be erected on the site immediately to the left of the old house.

40. Many will recall the sunken garden at the rear of Eastgate House Museum as it appeared before its recent transformation. This view was taken shortly after the opening, in 1923, of the 'Foord Annexe', on the extreme right of this picture. The garden, which together with the annexe had been designed by Sir Guy Dawber, RA, has now been levelled, and the flower beds and lily pond redesigned. Although still popular, especially with visitors, the garden has lost some of its character and its feeling of unity with the house itself. A prominent feature today is the chalet which once stood in the garden of Charles Dickens' home at Gads Hill Place, and in which the author did much of his later writing. It now adorns the open space between the main house and the annexe, where stands the large tree in this view.

41. The sun shines down from a cloudless sky, and life goes on at an unhurried pace in this everyday scene which in its way typifies our view of the world as it was around the turn of the century. It matters not that the carrier's wagon occupies almost half the width of the main road to Dover, or that the carriage bearing the army officer has to steer a course down the centre; the day of the motor car, or even the tramcar, has not yet dawned. Nevertheless, the passers-by in this picture would still recognise the scene. The buildings, happily, are little changed today, although one may now wine and dine where once Mr. Seeley furnished ladies with their drapery requirements.

ROCHESTER, OLD HOUSES.   E.T.W.D.

STAR HILL, ROCHESTER.

42. Trams first entered Rochester on 22nd December 1904, when the service was extended from the Chatham boundary along New Road and down Star Hill to its junction with High Street. Although the routes were laid out and owned by the City Corporation, the lines were leased to the Chatham and District Light Railways Company, one of whose cars, No. 39, is seen descending Star Hill. One of ten cars built in 1907, these and forty similar open-top trams maintained a network of routes throughout the Medway Towns, until replaced by motor buses on 1st October 1930.

43. This view, also looking down Star Hill, can be dated to about 1905. By then the tram lines had reached the bottom of the hill but had not yet been laid in the High Street beyond, or in Victoria Street on the left. The car seen here at the terminus is about to return to Chatham using the crossover in the foreground. The stone portico on the left once graced the entrance to the Theatre Royal where Charles Dickens made his childhood acquaintance with the theatre. The site is now occupied by the Conservative Club and the portico itself has, in recent years, fallen victim to a road widening scheme. The G.P.O. now stands on the empty site behind the railings in the High Street. The almost total lack of traffic and people is in complete contrast to the scene today at what is one of the city's busiest road junctions.

St. Bartholomew's Hospital, Rochester.

44. St. Bartholomew's Hospital was founded in 1078 A.D. by Gundulph, the 29th Bishop of Rochester, just twelve years after the Norman Conquest. It was situated outside the city walls because it housed people suffering from the very contagious disease of leprosy. It even had its own small chapel, which can still be seen adjoining the High Street. The lepers when walking in the adjacent fields had to ring a bell which they wore to warn unwary citizens. The present building dates from 1863 and with some additions and modernisation over the years is still in use and serving the needs of the city and surrounding area.

NEW ROAD, ROCHESTER.

45. Another view of St. Bartholomew's Hospital, this one taken from a point very close to the Rochester and Chatham boundary. This picture dates from the 1920s when New Road was still a relatively narrow tree-lined avenue. However, since it forms part of the main London to Dover road, it is nowadays much wider and very much busier. The ornate gas lamps and most of the trees have given way to functional electric light columns, and the occasional passing tram to a continuous stream of motor traffic. A large building providing accommodation for the hospital's staff now occupies part of the site on the corner of Gundulph Road.

46. Standing in the High Street at the point where Rochester meets Chatham is the little Chapel of St. Bartholomew. Built by Bishop Gundulph in 1078 to serve the leper hospital which he had also established, it was supported by the Priory of St. Andrew until the Reformation. By Elizabeth I's reign the chapel had fallen into disrepair and was leased to a George Hope Smith for 99 years on condition that he make 'the said Chappell (being old and ruinous and like to come to utter decay) to serve for an honest and seemly dwelling house'. By 1699 it contained two lower and two upper rooms, but it later reverted to a place of worship and by 1896 its restoration by Sir George Gilbert Scott was complete. This early photograph shows the Norman apse, the oldest remaining part of the chapel, with one of its three narrow windows. The Victorian wall paintings have since been removed and by the early 1960s the chapel had been beautifully decorated and provided with modern lighting and heating.

47. An Englishman's home... These desirable residences seem to be vieing with the old castle for the most commanding position above the Medway Valley. Part of the building on the right of the picture is 'Satis House'. Having been extensively altered over the years its appearance belies its antiquity, for it was here in 1573 that the then owner, Mr. Richard Watts, M.P., was visited by Queen Elizabeth I during her stay in Rochester. 'Satis' is the word said to have been uttered by the Queen in order to describe Mr. Watts' hospitality. Charles Dickens later borrowed the name and applied it to Miss Haversham's home in 'Great Expectations'. Today the house is one of a number of buildings in the city occupied by the King's School.

Esplanade & Arbours under New Terrace Castle Gardens Rochester.

48. Although still a pleasant place to stroll, the Esplanade today is part of a busy traffic route and casual conversation in the middle of the road would be ill-advised! This Victorian view, however, shows the scene as it was shortly after the roadway had been constructed, using rubble from the medieval bridge which had been demolished in 1856. The balustrading beside the river had also come from the old bridge. The low building in the background was a public swimming bath, built by the Richard Watts Charity in 1880. It was replaced by a new open air pool nearby, shortly before the Second World War, although the building remained in place until the 1960s. In recent years more land has been reclaimed from the river and there is now a landscaped promenade on the right.

49. In days gone by almost every hilltop in and around the city was surmounted by a windmill. Sadly they have all now vanished, the last to go being Delce Mill, so called because it stood at the top of Burritt Street in the Delce Road area of the city. Operated by Glover and Son, corn and flour merchants, the mill fell victim to demolition contractors shortly after the Second World War, although its base remained in situ for some years after that. The site is now occupied by a council housing development of the 1960s. In the prevailing post-war mood of enthusiasm for re-development, the demolition of an ageing and redundant windmill seems to have passed off without much local concern. Had it survived just a few more years into a more conservation-concious age its fate might have been very different.

DELCE MILL—The Last in the City of Rochester.

Watts Alms Houses.

ROCHESTER.

50. These almshouses in Maidstone Road were built by the Richard Watts Charity in 1858 to provide homes for sixteen elderly citizens of Rochester. Built on the site of an old fever hospital, their ornate style was reflected in this even more flamboyant arched gateway fronting on to Maidstone Road. The almshouses remain, indeed they have recently been extended by the provision of a range of modern bungalows to the left of the main building, but the arches have long since vanished.

51. Although Rochester had made provision for the education of its sons ever since the foundation of a school by St. Justus around the year 604, the education of its daughters had not received a high priority. Changing attitudes to the education of females in Victorian England, however, made their mark and on 9th May 1888 the Mayoress of Rochester laid the foundation stone of a new school – Rochester Grammar School for Girls – in Maidstone Road. Much of the finance for the school was provided by the Wardens of Rochester Bridge. This photograph was taken shortly after the school opened, but in outward appearance the building is little changed today. The school has of course expanded and now many of the girls are housed in a new building about three quarters of a mile to the south.

FOORD'S ALMS HOUSES ROCHESTER   PHOTO E KELLY

52. Under the terms of the will of Thomas Hellyar Foord, a benefactor to the city who died in 1916, provision was made for the building of almshouses. A site to the south of the city was chosen and these buildings were erected around a large grassed quadrangle with an ornate bandstand in the centre, the whole complex fronting on to Priestfields, the road leading to the village of Borstal. The almshouses, accommodating ten couples and 37 single people were opened in July 1927 by Prince and Princess Arthur of Connacht. As well as these almshouses, Thomas Foord provided for the building of the annexe to Eastgate House Museum (now the Charles Dickens Centre). He had already financed the restoration of the cathedral tower and the erection of a new spire.

22082 Rochester. Priory Gate.

53. Lying just to the south of the cathedral is the 15th century gate (now usually known as Prior's Gate), built as part of a defensive wall to keep armed raiders out of the priory grounds and also to ensure the privacy of the monks. The upper room of the gate, obscured by ivy, was once used to house the cathedral choir school and the houses to its right form a block of seven known as Minor Canon Row and built between 1723 and 1735 to house the Minor Canons of the cathedral. Between 1884 and 1892 the second house in the row was occupied by Canon Arthur Thorndike whose son Russell and daughter Sybil both rose to fame, the first as an author, the second as an actress. This area today still retains the charm and peaceful atmosphere which is reflected in this photograph from 1904.

S:Margarets Church, Rochester.

54. High on a hill with a spectacular view over the Medway valley the tiny church of St. Margaret stood for over five hundred years serving the vast, mainly rural, parish to the south of the city. However, nineteenth century housing eventually engulfed the northern part of the parish and prompted the church's enlargement between 1823 and 1840. Only the tower of the medieval church remains. When this postcard was printed, at the turn of the twentieth century, plans were afoot to demolish the whole building and replace it with a Gothic edifice. These came to nought, however, and the church itself remains little changed to this day. The tower has lost its covering of ivy, the gravestones have been placed to one side and a lychgate now stands by the entrance on the right. St. Margaret's now serves as the Chapel of Ease for the unified Parish of Rochester.

55. This interesting view of the Rochester Cathedral bells was taken at the Croydon Foundry of Messrs. Gillett and Johnston, where the existing eight bells were sent to be recast in 1920 and increased to ten by the gift of two new bells (bottom row, far right) by Alderman and Mrs. Willis in memory of their son who had been killed in France. The expense of recasting the bell in memory of Dean Hole (bottom row, third from right), was borne by the officers and men of the U.S.S. Pittsburg, in memory of their visit to Chatham in 1920. The new bells were rung for the first time at the Foundry on the occasion of a visit by H.R.H. Princess Beatrice. They were returned to Rochester and rehung in the cathedral, being dedicated by the Dean, Dr. J. Storrs, at a special service on Saturday 14th May 1921.

J. RUSSELL
+ Sons.

56. John Reginald Harmer became Rochester's 101st bishop when he succeeded Doctor Edward Talbot in 1905. Born in 1857, Doctor Harmer was consecrated in Westminster Abbey in 1895, and for the next ten years served in Australia as Bishop of Adelaide. Active in the cause of Prayer Book reform, Doctor Harmer served one of the longest apostasies in the history of the Rochester Diocese, ill health prompting his retirement in 1930. When he took up residence at Bishopscourt he became the first bishop to live in the city since John Fisher in the sixteenth century. Doctor Harmer died at Instow, North Devon, on 9th March 1944.

57. This picture shows the rather ornately decorated front of the Old Palace, now known as Bishopscourt, situated in St. Margaret's Street. The house was left in 1674 by Francis Head for the use of the bishops of Rochester, but was not used by them until the 1920s. After the Reformation the bishops had chosen to live in other parts of the diocese, such as Bromley and Sevenoaks. The Old Palace was therefore let to other tenants until 1836 when it was sold by the Ecclesiastical Commissioners. About 1920 the building was extensively altered: the decorative work disappeared and additions were made to the front of the building making it almost unrecognisable today from when this picture was taken. It remains today the official residence of the bishop.

RESTORATION HOUSE, ROCHESTER

58. Situated in Crow Lane at the eastern end of The Vines, is the splendid red-brick Elizabethan 'Restoration House', so named because King Charles II stayed there overnight upon his return from exile in France on 28th May 1660. It is designed in the shape of an 'E' and the south wing (seen on the right of this picture) betrays the Dutch influence. Samuel Pepys visited the house in 1667 during his inspection of the Medway's defences following the disastrous attack by the Dutch fleet, and later it was portrayed as the home of Miss Havisham in Charles Dickens' 'Great Expectations'. Dickens called it 'Satis House', a name which he had borrowed from elsewhere in the city. The house is here seen from The Vines at about the turn of the century when it was still festooned with ivy. This has been removed in more recent times and the extensive damage to the brick work made good.

CHURCH PARADE
ROCHESTER
APR. 26.08
5

59. The Medway Towns' close association with the armed forces has meant that the military church parade has for long been a familiar sight in our streets. In this view members of the City of Rochester police force and a number of small boys bring up the rear of the parade as it passes St. Mary's meadow on its way back to barracks after morning service in the cathedral on Sunday 26th April 1908. Contemporary press reports tell us that the service was attended by contingents from the Corps of Royal Engineers, the Royal West Kent Regiment, the Royal Army Medical Corps and the Medway Squadron of Yeomanry. In keeping with the fashion of the time there is not a bare head to be seen, even the smallest child wears a hat, while some of the ladies are clearly keen to give their Easter bonnets another showing.

TEA GARDENS. GORDON HOTEL. ROCHESTER.

60. What the occasion is we do not know, but these rather sombre looking ladies and gentlemen are trying hard to relax as they pose for the photographer in the tea gardens of the Gordon Hotel. Are they staff or customers? The tables are not laid so perhaps it is a staff picture. 'The Gordon' had been a private residence but was enlarged and converted into a temperance hotel in the late 1880s, being named after the famous General Gordon of Khartoum. Though no longer dedicated to the cause of temperance, the hotel is still very much in business today. Fortunately it has not lost its Victorian character. Modernisation has been tempered with restraint and a number of interesting features have been retained, including a dog gate, designed to deter our canine friends from climbing the stairs.

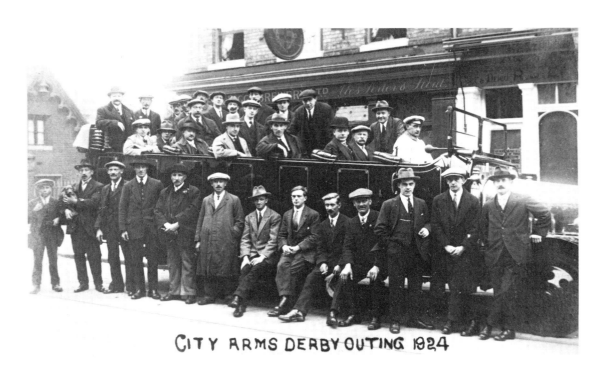

CITY ARMS DERBY OUTING 1924

61. The members of the City Arms Public House Sports Club are seen here posing for the camera early on the morning of Wednesday 4th June before departing for the 1924 Derby at Epsom. The delightful looking char-à-banc, which would be the pride of any museum today, is parked outside the City Arms in Victoria Street, whose host, Harry Jones, is seen in the front row, third from the right. The driver is looking somewhat apprehensive, perhaps he has a notion of events to come, for the day turned out very wet, the vehicle getting stuck in the mud on the racecourse for over four hours, after the race, and then getting lost in darkest Surrey, before the party finally reached home at 4.15 the following morning! It's not recorded whether any of them backed the winner, but for the record, Lord Derby's horse Sansovino won the 1924 Derby at odds of 9 to 2.

CITY OF ROCHESTER.

62. Excursion steamers had been a familiar sight on the River Medway since Victorian times, and the principal operator, the Medway Steam Packet Company, had been incorporated in the year of Queen Victoria's accession, 1837. Paddle Steamer 'City of Rochester' came into the company's service in 1904, joining 'Princess of Wales' on sailings to Sheerness and Southend. She is seen here, when still fairly new, rounding Gas House Point, Rochester, on her way down stream from Strood Pier. All Saint's Church, Frindsbury, stands high on its hill in the background but is overshadowed by the chimney of the Kent Electric Power Company's generating station.

63. After the First World War the company was re-constituted as the 'New Medway Steam Packet Company' and under the direction of Captain S.J. Shippick soon began to open up new routes, to places as far afield as Great Yarmouth and Boulogne, and to acquire additional vessels. In this view of the Port of Rochester with the cathedral in the background three members of 'Shippick's Navy', as it was affectionately known, can be seen lying at anchor. On the right of the group is the 'Medway Queen', built for the company in 1924, whose war-time adventures at Dunkirk have made her famous. She was the last of the fleet to remain in service, being withdrawn in 1963.

64. The coronation, on 22nd June 1911, of King George V and Queen Mary was of course attended by much public rejoicing, but since television and radio were not yet available to focus the nation's attention on Westminster Abbey, the event was celebrated at church services held throughout the land. In Rochester the Mayor and Corporation walked in procession to the cathedral for a service at which the address was given by Dean Lane. The Mayor, Councillor A.J. Knight, is here seen returning to the guildhall after the service accompanied by his mace-bearers. The bearer on the right is carrying the silver oar, symbol of the Mayor's office of Admiral of the River Medway. The dignity of the occasion, however, is lost on at least one young man whose main concern seems to be to get himself in the picture.

65. One of the duties of the Mayor and Corporation of Rochester has been the regulation of the fisheries on the River Medway. Oyster fishing was in 1865 a thriving industry giving employment to some 200 dredger-men. Although oysters are no longer harvested in the river, and the number of men who keep the Medway fishing industry alive has dwindled to a mere handful, the Court of Admiralty still meets annually in a boat at the Esplanade Pier. It is seen here in 1923, in the spartan surroundings of a sailing barge, with the Mayor, Alderman Price, presiding. On the left of the picture are three jurymen and a water bailiff. The Chamberlain of the Fishery, Mr. Hill, stands opposite the Mayor with the Town Clerk, Mr. Kennette. The macebearers and other officials observe the proceedings from a somewhat precarious position above.

66. The right to hold fairs and markets in the city is enshrined in the ancient charters and by the nineteenth century the cattle and produce markets had come together on this site in The Common. Taken on a quiet day this view shows the cattle pens with, in the centre background, cottages in Davis Square and, to the right, the embankment of the London, Chatham and Dover railway line. The grey bulk of the new Corn Exchange, built in 1870/71, looms over the buildings in The Common on the left of the picture. This thoroughfare was later to be widened and incorporated into the road now known as Corporation Street. Alas the cattle market is no more, but a thriving general market is still held here on Fridays with an antiques fair every Saturday.

67. Mechanical power versus horse power as seen here in this view of Corporation Street looking towards Rochester Bridge in the nineteen twenties. The brick arches of the Dover railway line form a backdrop to the Co-operative Wholesale Society's motor delivery van, while the two horse-drawn carts are standing outside the walled entrance to the 'Co-op's distribution depot, above which can be seen the cupola atop the guildhall. A couple of steam traction engines complete the picture, products, no doubt, of the local firm of Aveling and Porter. Behind the engines stands the City Restaurant and Tea Rooms, bastion of the local temperance movement. Corporation Street was built as a relief road when trams began running through the High Street to Strood in 1908. It is now a dual carriageway road and much altered from this view.

The Vines Rochester 1894

68. The Vines lies just to the south of the old walled city and as its name suggests was once a vineyard, attached to the Priory of St. Andrew. In more recent times it was the setting for Edwin's courtship of Rosa Budd in Charles Dickens' mystery 'Edwin Drood'. In Dickens' time The Vines was a lonely, slightly forbidding place, far less attractive to the casual stroller than it is today. However, in 1880 the Corporation of Rochester leased it from the Dean and Chapter and laid it out as a public park. This view, taken from the corner of East Row and Maidstone Road, shows the avenue of Plane trees, then over twenty years old with, in the centre of the picture, the 'Seven Sisters', which for safety reasons had to be felled in the 1960s. Many of the Plane trees were themselves destroyed in a great storm which swept across south-east England in October 1987.

69. Alderman Charles Willis is here seen being installed as Mayor of Rochester in the guildhall on 9th November 1908. This was his third term as mayor, he having previously held the office in 1906 and 1907. He was to be elected for a fourth term in 1909. The newspapers of the day reported Alderman Willis's acceptance speech, in which he spoke of unemployment as being the major problem in the area, aggravated by the recent closure of a number of cement factories. He hoped that the city's good transport facilities would encourage investors, including foreign companies, to move in and open up new businesses. Such sentiments have a familiar ring to the citizens of Rochester in the 1980s. The guildhall looks much the same today as it did in 1908; the many fine portraits, including those of King William III (left) and Queen Anne (right), have now been beautifully restored.

70. An unexpectedly high tide on the afternoon of Tuesday 1st November 1921 drowned large parts of the Strood side of the city under several feet of muddy water, as the River Medway broke its banks. Flooding extended inland as far as the Angel public house at the bottom of North Street, whilst this view of the High Street taken from the railway bridge, shows the aftermath looking towards Rochester Bridge in the middle distance. At the Victory Public House, farthest building on the right, the cellar was flooded and beer barrels floated up to the ceiling, whilst next door at Joseph Collis, the ironmongers, great damage was done to the stock. In recent years all the buildings on the left have been swept away to make the dual carriageway approach road to the widened bridge, whilst improved drainage and new river defences have lessened the risk of flooding.

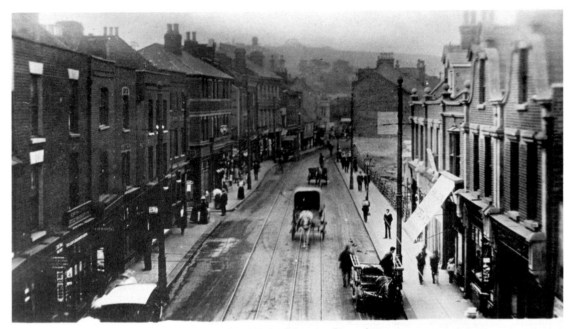

4031 High Street, Strood.

71. Strood High Street again, but this time looking towards the Angel Corner. Not a tram in sight, but plenty of horse-drawn traffic and shoppers casually strolling about in an age just before the motor car was to change all that. The clock on the left, something of a landmark, is above 'Fehrenbach Bros.', jewellers, before they changed their name during the First World War, to the more English sounding 'Fernbank's'. As in the preceeding picture, road improvement schemes have taken their toll and all those shops to the left of Fernbank's have since vanished. On the opposite side of the road, the vacant site awaits the building of the Invicta Picture Palace, which opened in 1919 but is also now no more, the site having reverted once more to shops. Despite its many changes the area remains a busy shopping centre.

St. Nicholas Church, Strood.

72. The earliest known church in Strood is believed to have been built about 1122 and was a chapel of ease to the Parish of Frindsbury. A separate parish of St. Nicholas was created in 1193. By the early part of the nineteenth century the building had fallen into disrepair and its demolition was ordered. A new church, incorporating the tower of the old, was opened on 9th October 1814. This view, from Strood High Street, shows how the church looked at about the turn of the century. The ivy and most of the gravestones have now gone, but otherwise a photograph taken at the same angle today would reveal little change. The changes that have occurred are mostly internal to fit it for its present dual role, as a place of worship and social centre for the elderly and disabled.

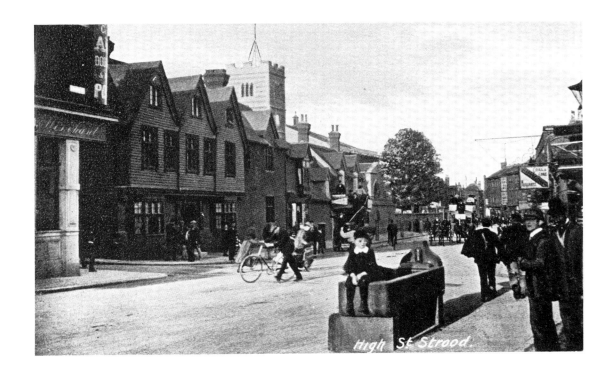

73. The tower of St. Nicholas' Church dominates this 1905 view of Strood High Street. The Elizabethan timber and gabled building at the corner of Gun Lane was demolished in 1927 to enable the junction to be improved, the fine panelling from one of its rooms being preserved in the city's Eastgate House Museum. In the foreground the small boy sitting on the horse trough is obviously more intrigued by the cameraman than in the mundane goings-on in the street behind. Several horse-drawn omnibuses are seen plying between Strood and Chatham and a man pushing a bicycle wanders across what is now a very busy road intersection.

74. Temple Manor, on the Strood side of the River Medway, was founded in about 1160 and takes its name from its early association with the Knights Templars. After the dissolution of the order in 1312 it passed to the Knights Hospitallers of St. John of Jerusalem. King Edward III conferred the manor upon Mary, Countess of Pembroke, from whose ownership it became the property of a monastery in Cambridgeshire. It passed into private hands after the Reformation. The manor house dates from the thirteenth century when, because of its closeness to the London road, it probably served the Knights Templars as a lodging house. This peaceful rural scene is now, alas, but a memory: the house and surrounding land were acquired by the City Corporation in 1930 and the house, albeit beautifully restored and cared for by English Heritage, now sits uncomfortably in the centre of an industrial estate.

GADS HILL PLACE, NEAR ROCHESTER.

Copyright

75. Not far from Rochester, in the village of Higham, stands Gad's Hill Place, a substantial house built in the late eighteenth century for a man named Stevens, a humble ostler who rose to become Mayor of Rochester. The house, which is now a girls' school, was seen and admired by the young Charles Dickens whose father remarked, prophetically, that if he grew up to be a clever man he might one day own it. John Dickens' prophecy came true and Charles acquired the house in 1857. He spent the closing years of his life at Gad's Hill and from there would often stroll into Rochester to wander the streets that had become so familiar to him as a child, returning to continue his writing in the little chalet which stood in the garden. Dickens died at Gad's Hill on 9th June 1870 and was interred in Westminster Abbey, despite his own and his family's wish that he be laid to rest in Rochester.

76. Cobham Hall, formerly the home of the Earls of Darnley, is approximately five miles west of the city. This view shows the west front, with the central block and adjoining wings set at right angles each with an octagonal turret which all date from the late sixteenth century. The central part of the Hall was rebuilt in the mid-eighteenth century, it is thought by Inigo Jones and John Webb, whilst at the end of that same century more alterations were carried out by James Wyatt. The grounds were landscaped by Humphrey Repton and his son John and there was a large deer park. Today this fine building houses a public school for girls and is open to the general public at certain times. The estate once extended right to the edge of the city, at Strood, large parts of it being acquired by the Corporation for development before and after the Second World War.